D0794047

Dear Parents and Educators,

This book is perfect for a **Progressing Reader** who:

- can figure out unknown words by using picture and context clues;
- can recognize beginning, middle, and ending sounds;
- can make and confirm predictions about what will happen in the text; and
- can distinguish between fiction and nonfiction.

Kate & Pippin

LEVEL 2

Encourage children to select books based on interests, not reading levels. Read aloud with children, showing them how to use the illustrations for clues. With adult guidance and rereading, children will eventually read the desired book on their own.

Here are some ways you might want to use this book with children:

- Talk about the title and the cover illustrations. Encourage the child to use these to predict what the story is about.
- Discuss the interior illustrations and try to piece together a story based on the pictures. Does the child want to change or adjust his first prediction?
- After children reread a story, suggest they retell or act out a favorite part.

PENGUIN YOUNG READERS
an imprint of Penguin Canada Books Inc., a Penguin Random House Company

Published by the Penguin Group
Penguin Canada Books Inc., 90 Eglinton Avenue East, Suite 700, Toronto, Ontario, Canada M4P 2Y3

Penguin Group (USA) LLC, 375 Hudson Street, New York, New York 10014, U.S.A.
Penguin Books Ltd, 80 Strand, London WC2R 0RL, England
Penguin Ireland, 25 St Stephen's Green, Dublin 2, Ireland (a division of Penguin Books Ltd)
Penguin Group (Australia), 707 Collins Street, Melbourne, Victoria 3008, Australia
(a division of Pearson Australia Group Pty Ltd)
Penguin Books India Pvt Ltd, 11 Community Centre, Panchsheel Park, New Delhi – 110 017, India
Penguin Group (NZ), 67 Apollo Drive, Rosedale, Auckland 0632, New Zealand (a division of Pearson New Zealand Ltd)
Penguin Books (South Africa) (Pty) Ltd, 24 Sturdee Avenue, Rosebank, Johannesburg 2196, South Africa

Penguin Books Ltd, Registered Offices: 80 Strand, London WC2R 0RL, England

First published in Puffin hardcover by Penguin Canada Books Inc., 2012. Simultaneously published in the U.S.A.
by Henry Holt and Company, LLC, 175 Fifth Avenue, New York, NY 10010. Published in this edition, 2015.

1 2 3 4 5 6 7 8 9 10

Book design by Patrick Collins/Véronique Lefèvre Sweet
Manufactured in China

Library and Archives Canada Cataloguing in Publication data available upon request to the publisher.

ISBN 978-0-670-06931-6 (hardcover)
ISBN 978-0-14-319346-3 (paperback)

American Library of Congress Cataloging in Publication data available

PENGUIN YOUNG READERS
LEVEL 2
PROGRESSING READER

Kate & Pippin

An Unlikely Friendship

Martin Springett
Photographs by Isobel Springett

This is Pippin.

She is a fawn—a baby deer.

Pippin waited alone in a field
for three days.
Her mother did not come back.

This is Kate.

She is a Great Dane.

Kate was sleeping in her dog bed.

She woke up and saw a fawn next to her!

Kate's owner, Isobel,

had found Pippin

and brought her home.

Kate nuzzled little Pippin.

She gave her a lick.

Pippin snuggled up close to Kate.

Kate had never had her own puppies,
but she was a gentle dog.
Isobel knew that Kate
would take good care of Pippin.

Pippin had to learn
how to drink sheep's milk
from a baby bottle.
At first, she bit the bottle
and was frustrated.
But after two days of practice,
Pippin drank.

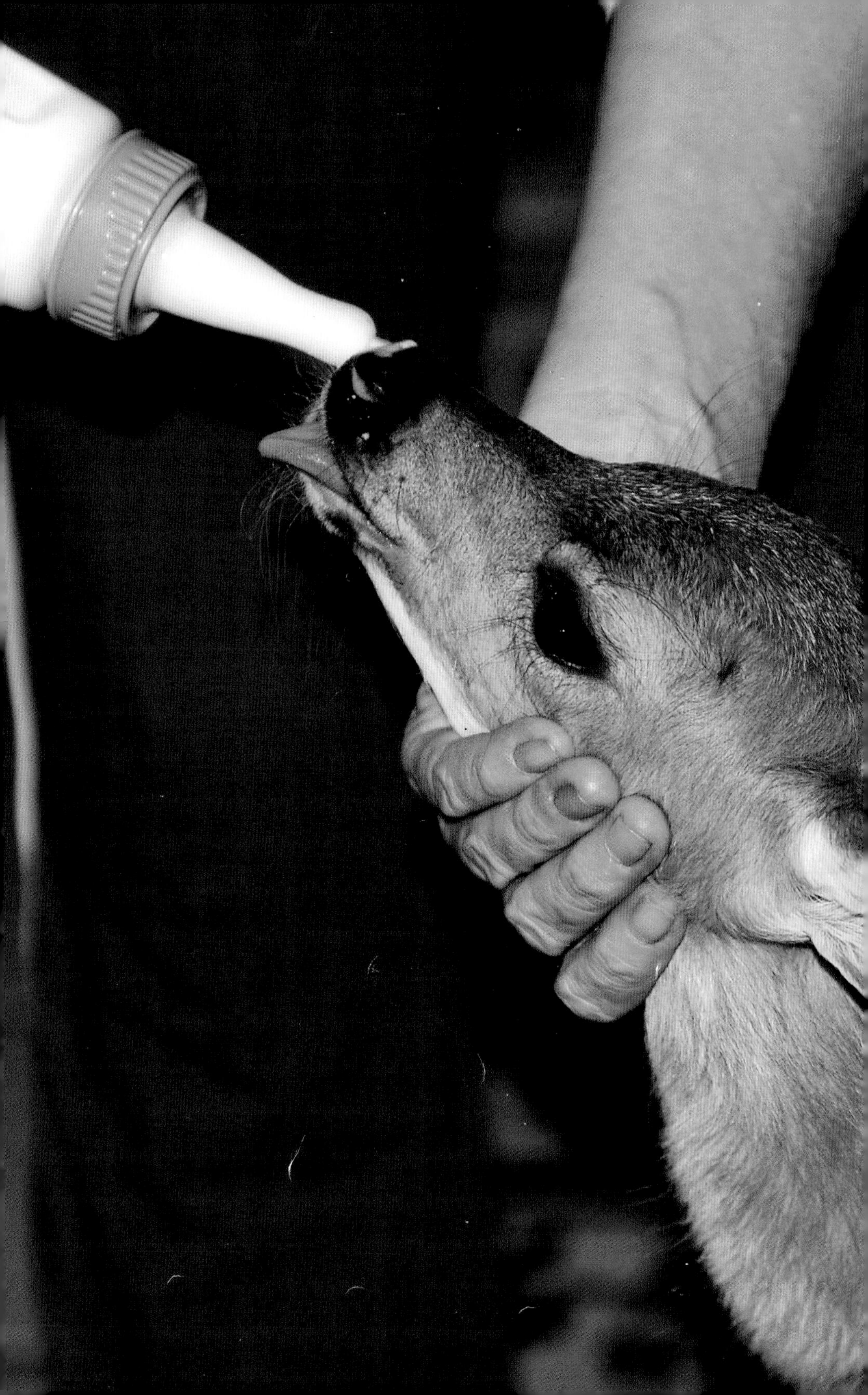

Pippin followed Kate everywhere—
just like a puppy
would follow its mother.
Pippin stayed inside for a week
so she could grow strong.
Then she followed Kate outside.
She figured out
how to climb down the stairs.

Now Kate and Pippin could play outside!

They ran around everywhere
until Kate needed a break.

One day, Pippin ran off.

Isobel called for her.

Kate waited for her to come back home.

They did not see Pippin that night.
Kate and Isobel worried
they might never see Pippin again.

The next morning,

Kate and Isobel both woke up early.

They waited.

Finally, at the edge of the trees,

there was Pippin!

Pippin came to greet Kate.

And she wanted some food.

After that, Pippin slept outside
in the forest every night.
And every day,
she came back to play with Kate
and eat snacks like bananas and bread.

Pippin grew up quickly.
The forest was her home,
but she still came to visit.

She even became friends
with Henry the cat.

But she was still Kate's little pup.

Some time later,
Pippin brought visitors with her—
two little fawns of her own.

Now Pippin was a mother.

And Kate was a grandmother!

Pippin's babies did not come
into the house.
They did not meet Kate or Isobel.
They stayed wild.

But they were content to watch while their mom spent time with her family.

Kate did not go near Pippin's fawns.

Kate knew not to get too close
or she might scare them away.

Even though she was a mother now,
Pippin still liked to play with Kate!
And she still liked to give Henry a bath.

Years later,

Pippin still visits Kate almost every day.

Pippin is a wild animal

and her home is in the forest

with her babies.

But Kate and Pippin

remain the best of friends.